In Fri

Ravi Sharma
11/09

A Collection of Poems

Pankhuria

By

Ravi Sharma MD

authorHOUSE®

AuthorHouse™
1663 Liberty Drive
Bloomington, IN 47403
www.authorhouse.com
Phone: 1-800-839-8640

First published by AuthorHouse 9/24/2009

ISBN: 978-1-4490-2975-3 (sc)
ISBN: 978-1-4490-2990-6 (hc)
ISBN: 978-1-4490-2991-3 (e)

Library of Congress Control Number: 2009909613

Printed in the United States of America
Bloomington, Indiana

This book is printed on acid-free paper.

To my daughters

Anuradha, Shobha and Geeta

Table of Contents

Few Words and Acknowledgement

Last year I published my poem book 'Pankhuria' in Hindi then I realized that many members from my own family and my own friends were not able to read Hindi. This prompted me to translate the poem book into English for a wider usage by the readers. I was fully aware of missing out on capturing the real sentiments and emotions conveyed in the original Hindi poems during the translation but it was still worth the try. I am not shy in accepting that some of my poems appeared to have improved in style with English translation, just to mention a few such as 'Beggar', 'Tsunami' and 'Haath Uthakar'. I have also tried to translate the titles of the poems in English to make it easier for the readers. For example, Pankhuria means petals and feathers, which reflects that the collection of my poems is like picking flower petals and feathers.

In my Hindi book of poems I had my watercolor paintings and the poems were printed on the same pages as the poems. I have been getting advice that I should also have my English translations printed over my paintings. I hate to disappoint the readers for not including painting for this book of translation. What I have done is that I have included about five illustrations in black and white and have included to the poems of English translation.

I am thankful to Indu Maitra who very kindly went over my translations and helped me in editing them. I am also immensely in debt to my friends Venkat and Jayanti Venkataraman for helping me out in setting the layout for the book with illustrations. I thank them for giving me hope for getting the book ready for publication. I would also like to thank my publisher Author House who helped in transforming my poems in the form of a book. I hope for the readers to enjoy reading the book of poems that covers diverse topics related to emotions, events and human relationships.

I would like to thank my wife Shashi and our three daughters Anuradha, Shobha and Geeta along with their respective families for bearing with me during long hours of absence from family gatherings. My special love is to my three granddaughters Shanti, Maya and Tara for being my princesses and my inspiration.

Ravi Sharma
Pittsford, NY
Date: May 2009

Unfortunate (Abhagin)

She got married at tender age
And gave birth to four
Two were taken by gods in bribe
So two could survive
She was consoled at that score,

She was wrapped in rags
Unable to hide her inviting youth
She was dazed in euphoria
Foolish but tenderly scattered her youth,

Her young body was used for a cause
Customers bargained often
Her youthful body when started to soften
She wondered when it would turn into ashes
A life like a corpse
When will it become a corpse?

AIDS

The son spoke to his mother
Ma please forgive me
A few years ago
I did not realize my blunder
For that reason
I must have to go
And go far away forever
Today I have betrayed
When I realized I had AIDS
On his sunken cheeks
Tears were rolling down
Ma only once
If you can
Hold me to your bosom,

Mother kept crying
She kept on thinking
How handsome her son was
How naughty her son was
Liked by all
And made everyone laugh
Why then?
No one knew.

Akarshan Pal Bhar Ka (Infatuation)

She was sitting with someone
At the front table
Laughing and smiling
Teasingly beautiful and awesome
Looked fresh and young
Removing locks of hair from her face
I fell for her loving grace
I was consumed in her wholesome,

She sensed from my glances
And withdrew a little
Only smiled and laughed still
She felt uneasy and not take chances
Removing locks of hair less often
For moments when our eyes met
With a throbbing heart I was all smitten,

How much I wished to meet her
To know all about her
I was lost in her thoughts
When I looked up
She was not there
I went out to look for her
But she was nowhere.

Talk (Baat)

His talk went straight to my heart
It pierced my chest and stayed there
It began to rise like a storm
Yet unknown it turned into a tear,

It affected my mind
The bitterness took over my heart
My forehead twisted with anger
Yet unknown it lit my eyes into a fire,

It can set fire and no smoke will rise
It can burn and no ashes will realize
It gives bitterness to the tongue
Then talk about bitterness in the talk
It surely gets stung,

His talk went straight to my heart
Yet unknown it turned into a tear
My forehead twisted with anger
Yet unknown it lit my eyes into a fire.

Balaatkaar (Rape)

Before the sunrise
Quietly she got up
Restless and tense
Stretched her arms and walked out
She yawned and let a soft moan out
Lost in her thought
Somewhere nearby she sat
Her head was bare
With Entangled hair
Her clothes were in disarray
She had no smile on her to carry
A soft blow of wind
While kissing her face
Reminded her of last night,

Her lips were partly open
She caught and bit her lip
And ran her tongue over to moisten
She stared blank into the emptiness
Helpless and searching the darkness
Wrinkles marked her forehead with strain
The tears welled up in her eyes in pain
A storm rose and then fell
In this turmoil the time could not be held
In anger her soft body would burn
Wet sweat on her neck would return
She would brush her face a lock of hair
And ask a question in despair
Not finding an answer
She became restless and more
With agony in her heart
She started questioning even more
About herself and her husband
Their relationship as pure
She asked
Then why rape
Why?

Barf (Snow)

Trees were silent and standing
Branches were white
And thinking
About the morning,

Trees were covered with snow
Shivering in the night
And thinking
About sunrise they want to know,

Branches were heavy with snow
Almost to the ground touching
And thinking
About bearing the weight of snow,

Mountains were covered with snow
All painted white
And thinking
About how long will it snow?

Trees are asking the falling snow
Where do you come from?
And thinking
If you are coming from sky
Where Sun is close by
Then why do you not melt away?
And still thinking
But were silent
Snow covered trees
Shivering in cold
Waiting for the morning
And thinking she is on her way.

Baykhbar (Unaware)

I simply lost my heart to her
And she was not even aware
She took my heart and walked away
Without a 'thank you' or even care,

I knew she was arrogant
But I have no complaint
By nature I am very patient
Only if she has no time constraint,

I wished I were the only one she loved
But many others are in love with her
I get very jealous over this
Perhaps she is not aware of this,

I had spent many nights with no sleep
Dreams do not come to me anymore
How do I console a lovelorn heart?
Who is not ready to listen anymore?

I simply lost my heart to her
And she was not even aware
I can't call her faithless and cruel
When she is all in the clear.

Bhikhaarin (Beggar)

She was a beggar
Lest she was mad
Draped in rags torn
She roamed the streets around
Helpless of her youthful form
Bursting out of scanty garbs
Unable to hide her youth abound,

She used to cry with hunger
Society looked down upon her
Poverty was her destiny
Her youth became her enemy
Helpless of her exposed breasts
How unfortunate was she
Became a victim of someone's lust,

One day surrounded
by a small crowd
She left behind her young body
Mocking and laughing
at the society
Unaffected by its prejudices
It didn't matter to her now
Whether it was just or unjust.

She was a beggar
Lest she was mad.

Bin Rukay Ansoo (Untamed Tears)

Thick clouds of dust
Arising from the ruins
Somewhere burning fires
Mixed with thick black smoke
In torn uniforms and with guns
Covered in blood were young men
Lying scattered here and there
Among the wounded and dead
A brother or husband, father or son
Family and friends keeping hopes
For tomorrow of a loved one,

Since the beginning of this Creation
When men were born
Violence was a solution
The world since has not changed
Violence is used for persecution
Causing unbearable agony
Has inflicted the pain
Thus knowing of the pain
It has touched the heart
Where there is darkness
In the midst and depth of gloom
The untamed tears
Ask why?

Bojh (Burden)

Prayed to God
Some day she would grow up
Just like others,

Who would know that?
She still remained a girl
Just innocent,

Her heart was soft
Like bees wax
Akin to a child,

Clever in her studies
Smart in talking
Just like the grownups,

Had a simple childhood
Suddenly had a surge
Like boiling milk in a pan,

Her childhood was scattered
Caused pressure on the heart
Like a river dam,

When agonized over path
Didn't know where to go
Like a lost traveler,

Winning for a gambler
Hope lurks around
Like cashing a counterfeit coin,

In her heart she desired
For a dry land's
Wish for a rain.

Bujha Deepak (Extinguished Lamp)

She brought the little girl
Wrapped in a blanket
Small innocent face
Somewhat lifeless
Droopy eyes half open
Heavy eyelids
Hurried shallow breathing
Body burning like fire
She was scared
With both teary eyes
With a beggar's voice
Folding her both hands
She wept and requested
Please doctor
Save my little girl
Her voice filled with agony,

The treatment was started
In clinic where girl was admitted
She had Lymphoma
Complicated by Pneumonia
There was some initial hope
Her progress was somewhat unclear
The effect of drugs had to bear
Prayers were trusted with hope
But fluttering of her lamp had started
It extinguished before it had lighted
If that was God's will
Then luck would follow 'His' will
The extinguished lamp
Remained extinguished.

Collar Ka Button (Collar Button)

Though nothing was unusual
I still could not sleep
The job interview kept me awake
The morning I fell asleep
I woke up late
I knew I wasn't ready
For an interview I had to take,

I dressed up in a hurry
A missing collar button caused me worry
I covered it with a tie
During interview I kept holding my tie
My mind was a huge missing button
I knew I wasn't ready
For an interview I had just taken,

Lost the job due to missing button
I wasn't able to focus on questions
I could not help thinking
Except for the missing button
I blamed button for everything
Even then I could not sleep
I knew I wasn't ready
For the interview that gave me creeps.

Dair (Late)

I am not happy
That you come late
It has become your habit
To have me wait,

I too have worked I do not pretend
The issue is for you to understand
How long will continue
This void and baseless trend?

Please make a promise
You will try to push 'late' away
If tried sincerely
You can be on time everyday,

I am reaching a ripe age
Those days of youth are gone
Have some regards for me
Let us be together where we belong.

Dosti (Friendship)

Sometimes a friend
Becomes a stranger
Like the weather
You have changed my friend,

True friendship has no rein
True blessing is in love than in hate
Fragrance in Virtues I wish you can retain
Lessons in friendship I wish you can take,

Inner secret isn't seen from outside
Like the layers of the onion cover inside
Throw away the baggage you have carried
The rein put on friendship need to be buried,

When in friendship
The friend becomes a stranger
Similar to changing weather
Change in you my friend
Changed our friendship forever.

Ek Choti Si Nazm (A Small Verse)

A small verse for you
I shall try
If I fail to write
Disappointment will rise,

I cannot foresee
How can we even talk?
If old memories
Ever return and knock,

If you forget me ever
It will be cruel and awful
Try those memories and remember
You may remember them still,

Memories are not verses
Written on paper
Those can be erased
At your wish whenever,

Do not worry for the memories
How and when they were born
If I failed to write a verse
Perhaps because for a rhyme
That verse is surely gone.

Misunderstanding (Ghalat-Fahmi)

She came to my house on her own
Then avoided me and walked away
She took my hand and then let it lay
She then forged her anger with a frown,

She lifted her eyelids with tender
And lovingly stared into my eyes
Thus building my hopes, I wonder
Then for rudeness I was denied,

She called me to come closer
By indicating with her finger
She smiled playfully
And then said goodbye
Perhaps leading me to invite her,

She lit a fire in my heart
While peacefully she could live
Thus making a fool of me
She went her own way
That I couldn't believe.

Ghaayal (Wounded)

My heart hurts
How do I console it?
Hurt is shared
How can I then forget?

That life is for four days
Two days are already gone
The rest needs to be spent
How can I then spend the rest?

Since immune to hunger and thirst
A broken bond with my trust
Sleep is gone
How can you then accept?

I never thought before
The day would ever come to that
Whom I loved and made mine
How could I ever part?

Life filled with bitter taste
Causing hurt to my emotional state
Made it difficult to spend time
How could I afford respect?

My prayer to you is that
Avoid the damaging act
Let the love return
How can I rekindle that?

Girtay Sitaray (Falling Star)

My wish as a falling star
Not to be seen as an outcast
I am the falling star
Do not view this as my defeat,

As a star to succeed
Depends partly on my fate
But to change my fate
Rests solely on my belief,

To lift me as a falling star
Consider it as my prayer
For me to shine again in the sky
Consider it a right by my savior,

I am tired of being judged
Do not make a bargain
Once I did fall
But I am up again
As a star most treasured,

A falling star's wish
Not to be seen as an outcast
I am the star that's falling
Do not view this as my defeat.

Golf Ball

A fearless white golf ball
Round like unripe guava
Was waiting on the Tee
A club with large head
Like a lion's paw
Suddenly jumped at the golf ball
Lifted her up in the air
Threw her far and far away
Only to land on the fairway
Stunned but then rolled farther away,

No one felt sorry for her
No one picked her up for a hug
She was hurt and sad
To her surprise she was hit again
And was air lifted once more
Only to land again
For a few rolls more
Until mud was on her face
She could not see anymore
Some one then picked her up
She was crying like never before,

She felt good
When cleaned on a towel
And had a little rest
She sat down on the green
And felt somewhat shy
She saw a flag standing by
Where the flag stood was a hole
Without a warning
And to her surprise
Was pushed into that hole
For a birdie roll
In spite of such rude behavior

She heard people cheering
Why? She was not sure,

Now look at the other golf ball
That got lost in thick rough
After she hit the tree
Laid unconscious and unaware
Thought they looked for her enough
Nobody even care,

That was very sad
Since the Titiliest Provie one
She took pride being the best
Near hole number seven
Jumped into the lake
Was drowned and laid to rest,

Now a very scared golf ball
Was waiting on the next Tee.

Haath Uthakar (Raising Hand)

A Muslim patient
Mother of two in her family
Visited the clinic
For pain in her belly
Its cause I did not know
The fear in her eyes
It seemed to grow,

Her eating and nutrition
She made no effort for a keep
She continued to lose weight
Her bones were digging deep
Seeing her in this condition
I was losing my sleep,

After physical and full evaluation
The mystery wasn't solved
Treatment without satisfaction
And no improvement at all,

Cancer was then suspected
But was not proved
Now the suspicion was shifted
To her emotional mood
She lacked love and respect
At home she was denied
For causing all this hurt
Her belly pain was tied,

One day she carried a gift
She put the pen into my hand
Holding my hands
She said this
"With those hands you gave life
My husband took mine by raising his."

Halloween

The morning I woke up
I got a shock
Mother had passed away while asleep
Four days earlier she decided
To leave
And then left us
When I saw her
She looked to be asleep
I couldn't believe
Amma had passed away

Many years had gone by
Her memory returned
Because that was Halloween
And today was too
That was a Friday
And today was too

In the evening children's laughter
Wearing different make ups
As Witches or Fairies
And Superman or Spiderman
While going around the neighbors
'Trick or treat'
Filling bags with candies

How happy they were
How innocent they were
The meaning of New Life
Was clearly seen
Celebrating Halloween.

Ilteja (Request)

Your getting upset will hurt me
Your rejection will shatter me
I will not trouble you again
If only you love me more
I will change forever from before,

What is my fault?
I do not know
Why do I have to pardon?
I do not know
Is this my punishment?
I am tolerating it
Is this your pleasure?
I am living it,

How can I let go
The secrets of my heart
A few precious moments
I hold inside my heart
I cannot reveal them
The secrecy of this silence
You may not comprehend,

I wished I were not there
I wished the feelings in my heart
Were never born
I wished the loneliness I had
Was long gone
I wished the disgrace could finally part
Then again what about the dreams
They would not be there
If I were never born.

Inam (Reward)

Whenever there is smoke there is fire
One can burn without smoke or fire
I helped him and hugged him
He left and forgot me
My heart pained and my eye filled with tear,

Partnership with greed was formed
Values were ignored life was moved around
Nobody knows why he is so calm
Such is the life he will love to crown
In future those values he will aspire
Whenever there is smoke there is fire,

Why is there no justice in this world?
They say in the house of God
'There may be a delay but justice is sure'
Patience to tolerate is not there anymore
Punishment to the culprit he must endure
You may console in many ways you desire
Whenever there is smoke there is fire,

Experiencing the life when it is lived
Counting rewards and few happy moments
Stores and safe full of wealth
Is that the final result and purpose of life?
The real reward will come when life expires
Whenever there is smoke there is fire.

Jheel Aur Baadal (Lake & Clouds)

Bunch of white clouds
Peeking into the lake
Twisting in the lap of wind
Forming figures and shape
Of a princess or an old man
Bunch of white clouds
Playing hide and seek with the Sun
Often hiding
But then peek at the lake for fun,

Gusty winds dancing with trees
Birds flying in groups into breeze
But the lake is quiet and still
Unaware of happenings
The secrets of the past
Lie deep into the lake
But chooses to be calm at will,

Bunch of white clouds are gone
And there is no overcast
The night is new
The Sun has set at last
The lake is asleep and sound
Do not wake her up
Or make even a sound.

Kerwa Chowth (Hindu Festival)

Kerwa Chowth is celebrated
During the fall season
This again brings happiness
In the hearts of everyone,

A young bride observes a total fast
While she keeps him in her heart
From early morning she is preparing
Delicious food and all for sharing,

She wears flowers and jewelry
And dresses up in her wedding sari
She is overwhelmed with joy and excited
When she sees him return and united,

She does ceremonial adoration
Story of 'Gangor' she reads in preparation
After prayers to gods as offering
She offers moon a ritual watering,

At the end she breaks her fast
And seeks his blessings
From the beginning of this tradition
Love is the significance in this fast.

Ladlee Bettee (Darling Daughter)

She was the only daughter
Brought up with their love
Her father never showed anger
A mother's darling
Always affectionate to others
Like the fragrance of a flower
Won everyone's heart,

How happy she was the other day
When she passed her exam
Parents were proud of her
The only daughter of them
Her beauty was in her simplicity
Her smile was refreshing like flowers
Her heart was full of hopes
There was music in her veins
God had given everything to her,

She resisted a lot
For he was a foreigner
To whom she was married
With tears in her eyes
Her parent's only darling
Left her parent's home
Today the parent's own
Was shaken up by a weeping heart,

Her mother was thinking
When she gave birth to her daughter
She nursed her with her milk
Raised her with love and care
Same daughter would leave today
Her love would be put to a test
Why is this tradition a must?

Her father couldn't believe his eyes
The little girl had become a lovely bride
Those days were gone
When she used to ride on his shoulder
He used to take her to a fair
When she was sleepy and tired
He would carry and bring her home
Today the same little darling
Brought him teary eyes
He was unable to let her leave home,

With heavy hearts
Both were thinking
The love and care they gave her
Would she get that?
They would get worried
How would she live?
How would she sleep?
How would she run the house?

In two years abroad
She had a little boy
She became a mother
She was proud to be a mother
She gave unconditional love
To her little boy
Even then she felt lonely
As if her life had a void,

As time progressed
So did the void
She felt depressed
And lacked the motivation
She would cry with no hesitation
She would wake up late
And felt it was in her fate,

She would remember her parents
Her eyes would well up with tears
She would hold her boy to her bosom
Troubled by memories of her childhood
The love she got from her parents
She could not get from her husband
Only the criticism and rejection,

There was no love or respect
In abuse the husband react
She had no smile on her face
She felt an immense disgrace
Who to tell and where to go
What to do she did not know
Totally helpless she did grow,

She used to feel closed
Bound by darkness all around
Life seemed buried to the ground
What about suicide?
Then she thought of the little boy
She held him to her bosom
And got rid of the idea of suicide
From her body and mind
Darkness started clearing
To live again became possible
She felt strong in her heart
For little boy's sake
She wiped her tears
To live again,

She left her husband
For her self esteem and pride
For her freedom too
Broke her silence
And asked help for her life,

Today in her life's struggle
The helpers are with her
The little boy goes to school
She is a schoolteacher
She is free
She is happy
She has new hopes
For her son
For herself.

Ma Ka Shoke (Grieving for Mother)

My mind is numb
My heart is heavy
My eyes are empty
In this moment of grief
The time has stood still
The life has left the body
How can this be fair?
The one who gave birth to me
Is now laying on the pyre,

I cannot believe
Amma you are not there anymore
As if it is a dreadful dream
I cannot accept the reality
For it is not a possibility
How can this be fair?
The one who gave birth to me
Is now laying on the pyre,

To leave the emotional bond
Though helpless I have to move beyond
How will it be possible?
My mind is still numb
As if I lost everything
Why soul and body broke their bond?
I cannot understand
How can this be fair?
The one who gave birth to me
Is now laying on the pyre,
Life and death are born the same time
But death holds the body from its soul
If this is true as I am told
Then why not I feel a bit consoled?

My mind is still numb
My heart is heavy
How can this be fair?
The one who gave birth to me
Is now laying on the pyre.

Maafi (Forgiveness)

I wish to be yours
And you to be mine
I wish to remove mistakes
And put faith back in line,

I was the culprit you claimed
For no reason I was blamed
How long can I live with shame?
With the hurt I cannot live any more
Usually the hurt is felt on both score
Some I carry and some you do too
When peace and happiness are gone
Feeling of revenge creeps on
Life's purpose is different
Hence that be known,

Thus I would like to say to you
Try not to think it is all about you
Try not to presume
The thoughts and minds of others
Try to forgive others
And forgive yourself too
If you are able to follow these
You will be mine
And I will be yours too.

Man Ka Dukh (Anguish)

Meeting of two people
As if arranged by gods
Love between them
Like a gardner with his garden
Their innocent and raw youth
Blue eyes and fair complexion
Created in music
Completeness is the truth
As if devoid of imperfection,

Destiny is unknown
He tried to commit suicide
But was spared
He felt hollow inside
Living a worthless life
He could not comprehend
Why such a major setback
How this happened?
Such anguish
His heart was filled with pain
Heaviness and intolerable pain
Imperfect and incomplete
Betrayed of their dreams
The story of two lives
Meeting of two people
Struggling to reclaim.

Manushay Aur Bhagwan (Man and God)

God created man
Or is it the other way around?
This question often comes to mind
I may also like to remind
Nothing is resolved by this debate
For there is no end to this debate,

Without color or fragrance in a flower
Black bees will not even hover
With no moon or sun
Night or day will not happen
With no air or water
Man cannot survive forever,

Pride brought arrogance to a man
To look like a swan he wished
Instead became a crow when he finished
When God created nature
Man fell in love with matter
O' fool, what is there to ponder?
Only God created the man
Nothing more is there to wonder,

The question often came to mind
I may also like to remind
That God created the man
Not the other way around.

Matbhaid Rang Ka (Color Discrimination)

I held her hand
To be with her
She shook her hand off
And walked away,

I tried to call her
She did not care to look my way
How easily she broke my heart
And walked farther away,

She was perhaps not aware
What she had done
I even thought
That I should block her way,

Wherever she went
I should go with her
And open my heart
To give it all away,

I asked her a few times
Why do you refuse?
Because I am black you are white
Color of the skin is all you sight.

The color I carry inside
She cannot see
It is not a secret
But this secret
Is known to her is hard to say.

Maya

This is just to let you know
This is only for you
We are thrilled
Excited and moved
Teary eyed
Your Nana and Nani
Welcome you
Our precious one
Oh ! MAYA
Thank you,

Our daughter's gift
Is a miracle
From God
Nana and Nani's dream
A little Laxmi
Is in our hearts
In our prayers too
Blessings to the precious one
Oh ! MAYA
Thank you,

You are beautiful and petite
Cute and complexion like wheat
Big eyes and round cheeks
Shapely full lips
A tooth trying to peek
Head full of black hair
Dimples in a cheek
We adore you
Our precious one
Oh ! MAYA
Thank you.

Mother's Day

You are a mother
And a Nani too
You are a wife
And a friend too
You are a lover
And a doctor too
But above all
You are a mother.

You have sacrifice
And little stubborn too
You have love in your heart
And service too
You live from within out
And confidence too
You are a bit sentimental
And cries too
But above all
You are a mother.

Whatever our mothers had
You have too
You remind me of them
And help me remember too
All the mothers should have
What you have too
You are made of sacrifice and love
And beauty too
But above all
You are a mother.

Mritu Daan (Euthanasia)

Birth
And Death
Are beyond one's own control
Time and control
End at the time of death
That's what I am told.

When he returned from Vietnam
His legs were paralyzed
He could not walk or even stand
And was confined to a wheel chair
His life was changed for worse
That he could hardly bare,

He demanded for his rights
And built his hopes
One after another hurdle in turn
Pulled away all the building ropes
His luck also laughed at him
Only brought more pain in return,

He was living a life of death
His health was on a decline
Hard for him to take even a breath
He was hooked to a breathing machine
He was still alert in his mind
To others he kept saying
"To kill your self would be a suicide
But euthanasia may be of some help
That may give some control to himself",

For the answer he did not wait
For permission he did not take
He turned the switch off the machine
And brought his death within his means.

Nace Bahu (New Bride)

Beautiful
Slim and fair
Tall and shy
A Gold medalist
She was the one who
One day became a new bride,

Traveled over the seven seas
She came this far
Full of excitement in her heart
She wasn't able to show
For parents house she just left
Where once she did grow
She was the one who
One day became a new bride,

She was simple by nature
Her mind was like a child
Laughing then getting upset
She could be playful beside
Reading, writing and sewing
That she very much liked
It was no surprise
To see her art always by her side
As grownups she stood tall
As the youngest she was called small
She was the one who
One day became a new bride,
She ran her shop and the house
She was a player of the team
She had confidence and courage
In her heart she carried a dream
She kept planning for future
Her life was blessed and fuller
Her sun was on the rise

When an eclipse moved in to hide
The time held her hands tied
She was the one who
One day became a new bride,

Her sun started setting
Darkness was increasing
Her dreams started falling apart
She still kept a desire to live and last
But God had planned a different path
When the time had an access
Darkness spread into her eyes
Her mind became more restless
In her heart the pain did occupy
But her sons love for her
And her husband's love
Made her fully aware
That she had them in her heart
Now showing on her face
She had total peace at last
Remember!
She was the one who
One day became a new bride.

Paimana (Scale)

They were close to us once
Are now distant and far away
The scale inside our heart
Weighed them as friends once
But that scale inside
Failed to measure the ideal way,

With ease they will say
They are close to them
And also to the others
But the truth really is
They are distant and far away,

The scale inside the heart
Cannot be scaled
Today it is not ours
Tomorrow it may not be yours
If you ask me honestly
Some friendships cannot be trusted
Then listen up my friend
Being close and distant
Has no real meaning anyway.

They were close to us once
Are now distant and far away.

Pal Ka Unt (End of a Moment)

Oh dearest one!
Stay few more moments
This moment must never end,

Like time of the dawn
The Sunrise must never end,
Oh dearest one
Stay few more moments,

Like inside dark clouds
The rain drops must never end,
Oh dearest one
Stay few more moments,

Like fragrance in flowers
Intoxicating bees must never end,
Oh dearest one
Stay few more moments,

Like in the heart of ocean
Rising waves must never end,
Oh dearest one
Stay few more moments,

Similarly, all your love in my heart
Heartbeat must never end,
Oh dearest one!
Stay few more moments
This moment must never end.

Palken (Eyelids)

I turned and looked back
She blushed and felt shy
With mischief she lowered her eyes
On her lips with concealed smile
She gracefully bowed her face
Instantly I fell for her grace
Our mutual transient silence we endured
And without a spoken word
The talk within our hearts was secured,

She lifted her eyelids with grace
With half opened eyes came to my face
Then lifted her eyes again
She looked into my heart
Before she lowered her eyes
I looked into her heart
I prayed
I saw a friend
One voice and
One heartbeat
She was hiding her face in hand
I turned and looked back
She blushed and felt shy again.

Pankhuria (Flower Petals & Feathers)

Dew drops shimmering in the morning sun
Trees are yawning and waking
Birds resting on their limbs
Fluttering feathers with their beaks
Butterflies waking the flowers
Half open petals and hovering black bees,

Here I am all excited
Threading my thoughts into my heart
And paint different colors
On life's huge canvas
My heart cries in jubilation
Only I had picked petals and feathers.

(Collection of my poems is like picking flower petals and feathers)

Patjhar (Autumn)

In the third quarter of the year
The Sun is less intense
The morning dew
And days are condensed
Evenings are dark and cooler
Wet and at times clear,

Many colors on the trees
Reminiscent of Holi
Grass covered with fallen leaves
Squirrels climbing the trees
And running on the dried leaves
Sounds pleasing to the ears,

Gusty winds bending trees
Robbing them of their leaves
Blowing them away and far
Once the trees with many colors
Reminiscent of Holi
Are now standing naked
With a promise
And heavy hearts.

Patnee (Wife)

It looks you are hiding something
'Cause you have a secret smile
Are you keeping a secret?
You are trying to hide,

I know you do trust me
Then share it with me
What is the matter now?
You secretly keep smiling
Obviously, you are enjoying
In teasing and annoying me
Then come and sit with me,

But lo, you are leaving
Where are you going now?
Why are you so stubborn?
That you are not sharing
Then keep your secret to yourself,

Now why is this anger?
You seem to be turning it around
For you it may look sound
And I am to be blamed
For calling 'East as West'
Now asking me for a pardon
For a blame that isn't just,

What is the matter now?
You are still smiling
And the reason for shyness
Is a secret
You are trying to hide.

Patthar (Stone)

A stone that is lifeless
Can take one's life
A stone with no brains
Can be called a 'god'
A man with no heart
Can be like a stone
O' stone let me ask
Why do you not have any love?

He who lives in the mountains
He who sleeps on the riverbed
Was free once but not anymore
Forced into raising buildings
And painfully chiseled into statues
Walls were built with him
Forcibly removed from his home
He was blown to pieces often
And was sold and traded
He was kicked in the streets
During the unrest
Was often used as weapon,

A stone that is lifeless
You are asking
Why doesn't he have any love?

Pitaji (Father)

I remember that day
When I lost you
It then happened
What I was afraid of
I knew one had to leave one day
But I refused to accept that anyway,

I have heard all those stories
When I was small
You started as a teacher
And earned Rs.30 a month
You carried that in your headgear
With that Amma helped the rest
And worked very hard
Cared for elders in the family
Even saved eight annas a month
That was how she managed the budget
Education was your priority,

You always respected Amma
And took care of her
No one ever heard
You raising your voice on her
You always helped Amma
In the household choirs
You followed the basics
And customs of the family of yours
We were blessed with those
And carry them today into ours,

From the time I became aware
I remembered those moments
Once you told me
'God is the cause of all the causes'
With your blessings

I walked on a path
It was a long journey
With your help I found my balance
I remember your coming to America
Your daily walks
And helping Amma learn American ways
You felt happy seeing greenery and flowers
You wondered how lucky the cows were
Who had plenty to graze,

You spent your time in volunteering
And became a doctor at age seventy
To give free treatment to the poor
As the president of Kailash colony
Helped in getting electricity and water
And made colony livable for others
With the use of a type writer
Remained active as an author
You enjoyed eating sweets
Who would I now buy the sweets for?
After the days tiredness
Who would be asking for a massage?
How eager you were to learn and read
Who would now read my books?
That habit of your long walks
Those paths would be empty without you
The path of life you had shown me
I would never forget,

I remember that day
When I lost you.

Prem Bandhan (Bond of Love)

To see butterflies and flowers
In a special bond of love
Are forever united
Given a choice of life of love
I would be excited,

Butterflies drink nector from flowers
Flowers in the garden are happy
They are laughing and feeling giddy
Wanting butterflies to be closer,

How playful butterflies are to feed
In hot sun and cold breeze
Flowers swaying in ecstasy
Calling butterflies are high
While tender young flowers concede,

Flowers give nector and fragrance
Butterflies in return pollinate the flowers
There is no distrust or discrimination
In a special bond of love
They are forever united
Then why not us in a life of love
Given a choice I would be excited.

Presume (Anumaan)

I presumed with open gate
Into a cloud of fog
I lost all reasoning
My heart throbs
For absolute Truth I wish to seek
Presumptions or Perceptions all I keep
Twisted foundations still persist
My mind is crowded
Like the coach of a train
My heart sags with hurt and pain
Beneath eyelids I hide tear
Also believe in what I hear
Though my thinking is confused
I continue to presume,

I feel anger into my gut
I believed gossips those I kept
I never forget or forgive thee
A strange and broken friendship
And me
I continue to presume.

Remembering Ahkhista Tragedy

Two promising boys
Brought parents lot of joy
Being ahead in the class was clear
Their humility was much to bear,

Voices from their Heart
Searched for a Meaning
But were lost
In pursuit of the Meaning,

Journey of All
Took a wrong turn
How could they recall
What Destiny had done?

That tragic dark moment
Spread a blanket of sorrow
Then Ahkhista gave her Heart
Whosoever could borrow?

Yearly visits to Ahkhista
At the Memorial
The ocean and grief
Sitting close to the ocean
Brings all so much relief,

I do not know
I DO NOT want to know
Whether 'This' is right
Or 'That' is wrong

But is enough for me
It makes me strong.

Saayaa Teraa (Your Image)

Your thought was in my heart
Your image I could see
To paint your image I had wished
Then your image I could not see
I closed my eyes your image I could see
I opened my eyes your image
I could not see,

I wished to have you in my dreams
I could neither sleep nor had dreams
Day and night I lived with your thoughts
Then I pity myself what have I got,

Your thought was in my heart
Your image I could see
I opened my eyes
You I could not see.

Seva (Service)

O' The Creator
You gave birth to me
But why was I put on stage?

After the rituals and sacraments
Question was raised
What is the significance of this life?
How does life differ from living?
This question raised more questions
Sense or lack of it couldn't be appraised
O' The Creator
You gave birth to me
But why was I put on stage?

In the search of self I lost myself
The right path couldn't be found
Life's purpose, living and fate
I could not get around
O' The Creator
You gave birth to me
But why was I put on stage?

Friends and foes taught me alike
Tuition to the teacher for learning I might
Significance of death weighed more than life
Hence the desire to serve came to mind
Service seems the real meaning to life
O' The Creator
You gave birth to me
To serve is why I was put on stage.

Shanti Jiji (Shanti Jiji)

"Where are you"?
Jiji called out
We still remember that day
The phone call came from India
News of the cancer
Our hearts sank
As if under our feet
The earth had moved
We wiped our tears
And called Jiji to return soon
Surgery and chemotherapy
Those treatments were tuned
Jiji went regularly for her therapy
Once again chemo and surgery
Jiji suffered night and day
She had courage all the way
Her love for the children
All she carried in her heart
We used to cry night and Day
Her unconditional love
And faith in God
That is why today
God made Jiji
A shining star in the sky.

Shanti

The morning our daughter became a mother
Outside the room and farther
First cry of the newborn came closer
Immense joy welled up our eyes with tears
We thanked the Lord for our prayers

O' Daughter, this gift from you
Wish for Nana and Nani has come true
Family of yours is now new
Since the addition of one to two of you

Her face is innocent and she is petite
Her wandering eyes and soft cheek
Her lips are wet and sweet
Her hair is light and eyebrow a streak

She has brought love and affection
Furthering ahead Sharma Hug tradition
Literally, she is Peace in entirety
She is our beloved SHANTI.

Suhaag Raat (Honeymoon Night)

She is sitting close
With her eyes lowered
Her head is bowed
A veil hiding her face,

Sari border inches down
From her shoulder
And Slips over her bosom
Drops and collects in her lap
Exposing her youth of a woman,

Jingling colorful glass bangles
Adoring her wrists
Her arms are delicate and long
Their desire is hard to prolong,

The night is still young
She is sitting close
With eyes closed
I held her face in my palms
Tenderly lifted to kiss her lips
She shyly turned her face away
Half of my lips slipped onto her cheek
Half rested on her lips in a loving way,

It's the night of the honeymoon
She is sitting close.

Tara

Plucked you from the sky
You became our own star 'Tara'
Most loved and special
Our princess Tara,

Since you have come to us
Our hearts twinkle with love
You we love, the special one
Our princess Tara,

When you laugh or giggle
That brightens us and our house
You the special one who is loved
Our princess Tara,

Long live our darling
We bless you from our hearts
You are loved and you are special
Our princess Tara.

Terrorist (Aatangwaadi)

If ever I met a terrorist
I would ask him
Why did you become a terrorist?
Why violence?
Or was it revenge?

You said
You were not free in a free country
Your land was taken away
You lost your job in a similar way
Emotional and physical hurt to family
You were treated with tyranny,

You felt
All the roads were blocked
Frustrated and confused
Your rights were refused
Revenge grew stronger in your head
Becoming a terrorist was the only step

Now In a security prison
You lost your freedom
But wanting to be free
You risked your life.
When trying to save it.

Tsunami

I have trust in God
Why not in His Creation?
God always means well
But Nature's fury you can never tell,

If God created Nature
Why can't He control it?
If God wrote our fate
Why can't we trust it?

When Nature adopted a horrid form
Tsunami was then turned on
That shook the bottom of the sea
And lifted huge waves it meant to be
For many thousands lives were lost
And millions lost everything they got,

Is this the working of God?
Or the Nature's fury
The Nature we can all see
But God where is He?
God is only a faith
And nothing more to me.

Tumhain Yaad Hoga (You Probably Remember)

You probably would remember
That we had met before
The day you were upset
I tried to help you for sure
But you remained upset
And were stubborn too
I gave up then on that score,

Your name was on my lips
You were in my heart
From your gentle hands
I received your tenderness
It seemed like an ecstasy
I was in heaven at last,

I looked alive from outside
But I was numb from inside
For this condition of mine
You did already sign.

How then you do not remember?
That we had met before.

Un Dino Ki Baat (Those Days)

It was during those days
When we were young
We were madly in love
Although we were two
But considered as one
At the time of the dinner
We shared the same bite
Also ate from one plate
If we did not share this way
We used to get upset
What did happen to us then?
We were lost in love.

It was during those days
When we were not so young
We still loved each other
But were not lost
Although we were two
And remained as two
At the time of the dinner
We did not eat the same bite
We shared
But ate from different plate
The leftovers we kept separate
And did not get upset
What had happened to us now?
We had found us in love.

Uttaijna (Excitement)

A humble momentary excitement
Arose in my heart
Not spontaneous and yet unknown
Broken fragmented and yet welcome
Into my heart

A content and infinite excitement
Suddenly turned wild
And filled my mind
It was unnecessary yet was not wrong
A humble passing excitement
Arose in my heart

Her
Agonizing heart
A lonely and reflective life
She swung between life and slide
Unable to find a balance
She struggled but did decide

Lo Behold
At last success filled her life
Looking at her now
I hide tears in my eyes
It might not be necessary
But was not wrong either
Familiar but lasting excitement
Arose in my heart.

Vaivhaar (Behavior)

Worshipping God in the idol
Is belief and your faith
The idol is a stone
Calling stone as 'God'
Has to be faith alone,

Giving birth without marriage
Call it a sin or a mistake
When love is blind
Leaves all values behind,

A man loves another and is gay
Women too go a similar way
Is this love or a lie?
Immoral some would say,

Sparing the weak and infirm
In war losing healthy young men
Call this stupidity or self-conceit
Or untamed behavior of man.

Varsha (Rain)

O' Cloud, rain, rain no more
Lest the river should overflow
O' cloud, roar, roar no more
Lest the village cows should fear,

The sky full of dark clouds
And the heavens split by lightening
A continuous downpour of raining
Lest the farm land should become a river,

Naked children playing causing uproar
The frogs croaking forever
Then again lightening and thunder
Lest the lightening should strike a tear,

When rain drops sound like ptr..ptr..
Street drains running and overflowing
Then again the fear of flooding
Lest washerwoman's house should become a sewer,

Lightening and thunder
Only makes loud noise and scare
When it is compared with the rain
Rain causes rivers to swell and swear.

Woh (That One)

I saw a beautiful smile
I saw a lovely gesture
I saw impeccable luster
But I never saw such eyes,

I fell for her beauty
Her shadow may mark her beauty
I never saw such elegance
Her graceful walk with pride
I never heard a sound of her stride,

Kiss of passionate love on her lips
I never saw such a mischief
It is merely the Creator's divinity
I never felt such an ecstasy,

Her face has such dazzling beauty
I never saw such display of character
She deserves a bouquet of flowers
I never saw such humanity.

Such a luster when I saw
But such eyes I never saw.

Yaadein (Memories)

While we were together
Our memories were made
When we were not together
Our memories did rejuvenate,

Your memories are pleasant
I remember them often
Yet my poor heart flutters
When I think of you with them,

Live by memories the choice we make
Since the life's journey is long
The power of time that's all it takes
The prediction for future we cannot make,

If only I could erase memories with magic
If only I could return your magic
If meeting again is not possible
Then to forget you would be impossible,

Memories are not verses written on paper
So you can erase them at your wish
They live here and there in your heart
Thus cannot be erased even you wish,

When our final time will arrive
Our soul will part our bodies
What will happen to our memories?
Will they bond with soul and survive?

Zamin (The Earth)

O' Earth how beautiful you are
Clad in a white shawl standing alone,

You are the 'Form' in Nature
The 'Feeling' of Divinity we adore
Like in the history books
You have been writing for centuries
Infinite secrets in store,

There is joy on your face
You offer poetry in the flowers
And for flowing love into rivers
We offer our gratitude for your grace,

O' Earth how beautiful you are
Clad in a white shawl standing alone.

Breinigsville, PA USA
27 October 2009
226519BV00003B/3/P